INSIDE

by Rosie MacPherson

Published by Playdead Press 2014

© Rosie MacPherson 2014

Rosie MacPherson has asserted her rights under the Copyright, Design and Patents Act, 1988, to be identified as the author of this work.

A CIP catalogue record for this book is available from the British Library.

ISBN 978-1-910067-26-0

Caution
All rights whatsoever in this play are strictly reserved and application for performance should be sought through Strawberry Blonde Curls via john@strawberryblondecurls.com before rehearsals begin. No performance may be given unless a license has been obtained.

This book is sold subject to the condition that it shall not by way of trade or otherwise, be lent, resold, hired out, or otherwise circulated without the publisher's prior consent in any form of binding or cover other than that in which it is published and without a similar condition including this condition being imposed on the subsequent purchaser.

Printed by BPUK

Playdead Press
www.playdeadpress.com

INSIDE was first shown on 11th July at the Lowry, Salford with the following cast:

ANNIE   Rosie MacPherson

Writer   Rosie MacPherson
Director   Ed Lilly
Producer   John Tomlinson
Set Designer   Celia Dugua
Sound Designer   Sam Skitt
Stage Manager   Ruth Burgon

STRAWBERRYBLONDECURLS
THEATRE COMPANY

Strawberry Blonde Curls was founded in 2010 by John Tomlinson and Rosie MacPherson, with their sell out regional tour of tragic-comedy Elastic Bridge. In 2013, SBC returned with their second original production, one-woman show Inside. Written and performed by Rosie MacPherson, Inside previewed at The Lowry and Theatre503 before a critically acclaimed run at Gilded Balloon as part of the Edinburgh Fringe Festival. The show opened its 2014 tour at the prestigious Canterbury Festival.

In 2014, SBC developed new show Century with the support of The Crucible Theatre, Sheffield which will tour in 2015. SBC are currently working on Tanja, which has been shortlisted for the Old Vic New Voices T.S Eliot Commission and Contact Theatre's Flying Solo commission.

www.strawberryblondecurls.com

Rosie MacPherson | ANNIE and Writer

Rosie is a Writer and Actress from the UK.

Rosie's work always has a strong human interest to it, drawing on real life stories that are often the subject of national and international press interest. "I believe very much that theatre and art are the voice to open discussion and raise awareness of issues such as feminism, immigration, politics, abuse, war and morality."

Rosie is currently writing her third play *Tanja*, which has been shortlisted for the Old Vic New Voices T.S Eliot Commission and Contact Theatre's Flying Solo commission. Set in Yarl's Wood Immigration centre and based on real life events. It is the story of one woman's bravery in the midst of prejudice and abuse. Rosie's acting credits include *Before I Go To Sleep* directed by Rowan Joffe (*28 Weeks Later*) for Scott Free Productions; lead roles in super-natural TV pilot *Border Queen* and British sci-fi feature *Run Away With Me*; *Doctors (BBC)*, *Ideal (BBC)*, *Emmerdale (ITV)*, *The Plantation (BBC, BAFTA Nominated)*, *What's The Story (C4)*, *Club Skin (Cannes Film Festival)* and *Powder (Theatrical Release)*.

www.rosiemacpherson.com

John James Tomlinson | Producer

John is currently the Assistant Producer at Sheffield Theatres, having completed a year as the Stage One Regional Producer. He is also the Associate Producer of *JB Shorts*, a Manchester based event that brings 6 new pieces to the stage from top TV writers. He recently worked with poet, writer and performer Ben Mellor (BBC Radio 4 National Poetry Slam Winner) and instrumentalist Dan Steele to produce and manage their ten-date tour of *Anthropoetry*, a fusion of spoken word, poetry and musical journey through the human anatomy.

John was part of Contact's Re:Con scheme for young producers and programmers and developed a 24 hour multi-platform arts event *24 Arty People* that created innovative work from all types of creative people. He is also an actor with TV and Theatre credits and graduated from University of Salford in 2009 with a First in BA (Hons) Media and Performance.

The setting is cold, dark and dingy.

> *A distant TV can be heard, with the occasional sound of footsteps. A heavy steel door stands menacingly tall. There is a rusty sink, cupboard, small dining table with two chairs and the remains of breakfast for two. A large free standing metal bucket - used as a bath and in the corner a nest of blankets used as a makeshift bed. An old camcorder is set up on a tripod. At the back of the cramped room is a dirty shower curtain - hiding an even smaller secret room.*
>
> *We are in a basement.*
>
> *ANNIE STOCKTON (24) lies in a crumpled heap on the floor, barely moving. She is pale and sickly looking. Her clothes are old and dirty.*
>
> *She groans as she struggles to sit up. She has been crying and has a bust lip. Clutching her stomach she labours to her feet. She leans on the table for support, trying to cope with her injuries.*
>
> *Suddenly, Annie scrambles across the floor to check something. From under her bed she pulls out a small shoe box. She strokes it before placing it back under the bed.*
>
> *She sits opposite the camera and turns it on.*

ANNIE: Mum, hope you and Jessie are OK? I did a bad thing. I don't know why I'm always so selfish, actually kidded myself into thinking it would be a nice surprise.

I try to be good and I always get it wrong. Have to try harder.

I know I can do better.

> *She must get on with her day. Annie starts to clear the table, making great effort to be quiet.*
>
> *She eats all the food on each plate, then dusts the crumbs onto the floor before putting them in the sink. BANG!*
>
> *A plate drops... Annie silently panics, scrambling to pick it up, glancing towards the ceiling. She waits a moment. Listens. Nothing.*
>
> *She struggles on, taking She a knife from the sink. Annie crawls under the dining table and scratches into the wood with the knife staring at the underneath of the table for a moment, before climbing out.*
>
> *Every movement is a struggle. She notices her bleeding lip and tries to lick it away - annoyed at the distraction.*
>
> *Taking a cloth from the sink, she wipes the table methodically. Up-down-side-to-side. Not good enough, she wipes again. Up-down-side-to-side.*

A sharp pain flares in her abdomen.

*Annie moves to the secret room and goes inside, carefully closing the door silently behind her - **we can't see her**.*

A short while after she bursts back out - obviously worried. She washes her hands at the sink. Counting as she does. Three wipes to the right hand, three wipes to the left. Scrub together three times and repeat. Every action prepared, controlled and familiar.

Annie opens every cupboard and drawer, looking for something else. She finds a tiny lump of cheese. She sits at the table, carefully and precisely cutting the cheese up. She sprinkles it on the floor.

She gets on all fours and looks through cracks and holes.

ANNIE: (*WHISPERING*) Mel B? You can come out. Look, some lovely cheese!

> *Still sprinkling the cheese, Annie moves cautiously away from the steel door.*

ANNIE: Told you not to go near the door Mel B. You turn to dust when you get electrocuted, like Debbie in Addams

Family Values. We DON'T touch the door and we DON'T press Eject -

Sharp pain hits her.

ANNIE: Where are you? I won't ask you again. We've all had our breakfast and it's just you that will have to go hungry.

Fine Missy. You go and live it up. Some of us have got things to do.

> *Snapping back into her routine, she walks to the metal bucket and fetches an old newspaper hidden beneath.*
>
> *She fetches a glass of water, sellotape and a potted plant from under the sink. Long-since dead, the plant is dry and dark brown, with sellotape holding it together. But Annie carries it to the table like a new born baby.*
>
> *She sits at the table with her newspaper and begins to water the potted plant.*

ANNIE: Morning Briony Petals my love. Good sleep?

Get that down you. I'll just fix your branch for you coz you've gone a bit wonky. It won't hurt I promise. Deep breath...

> *She secures the last remaining branch with sellotape.*

ANNIE: There you go. All done. Very brave.

Annie pretends to listen as if the plant is responding.

ANNIE: Don't be daft. You'd stick me back together if I needed it! You, me and Mel B - we're bezzies.

Not noticing the sound from above, Annie pats the plant and opens the newspaper, mimicking the grown-ups at the breakfast table with their daily paper. She flicks through until she finds the story she wants. Her reading level is that of a twelve year old.

ANNIE: No... No... No, ah.

A five-year-old British boy has drowned whilst on holiday with his family at a popular Spanish resort.

His grandmother claimed that her son and two holidaymakers had tried to resuscitate him without assistance from hotel staff. She said lifeguards had not been on hand and also claimed that an ambulance had taken four hours to arrive. Asked how the family was feeling, she said: "Heartbroken."

Awful things happen out there Briony. Even nice things like going on holiday.

Makes you think how lucky we are, down here.

Annie flicks some more pages.

ANNIE: Bowman was stabbed in the neck and stomach, and then raped as she lay dead or dying near her home in Croydon, South London, two weeks after her 18th birthday...

Annie looks to the ceiling.

ANNIE: He would never do that. Not now we're helping him fight the Evil Spirits. Int that right Katie?

She gets up and walks to the wall, next to her bed. She knocks on the wall and sits next to it. Talking to someone.

ANNIE: Don't want for nothing down here do we. Could be out there going off the rails.

She touches her bust lip.

ANNIE: Yeah I'm sorry you had to see that.

At least it doesn't happen that often now. Visit day isn't it...

Yep, 28 table scratchings. You know the drill, just be quiet.

And don't worry I'm OK, see!

Rather me than you. I'm used to it. .

Better make a move.

> *She taps the wall affectionately, stands and walks to the metal bucket.*
>
> *Annie takes off her t-shirt and leggings revealing blue coloured bruises all over her skin – some old, some fresh. She is insecure about her bare flesh and covers herself as she steps in the metal bucket.*

ANNIE: Nice hot shower to start the day...

> *But the water in the bucket is cold and makes her jump as she climbs in.*

ANNIE: Ugh! Mum! I'm in the shower, turn the tap off its making it cold!

Haven't got time for this!

> *She reaches into the steel bucket for more water, this time it has the effect of a hot power shower.*

ANNIE: That's better...

> *She sings.*

ANNIE: Stop right now, thank you very much. I need somebody with a human tooouuch. Hey you, always on the run, gotta slow it down baby gotta have some fuuuuun...

Annie pretends to soap herself up.

ANNIE: Lavender shower gel, lots of bubbles.

Lavender smells like old ladies, but you've gotta be mature to be taken seriously in this day and time.

She pats her face as if putting bubbles on her chin.

ANNIE: Bubble beard. Ho Ho Ho. (*IRISH ACCENT*) Some people say I look like me Da!

> *The pain strikes worse than before. She is disturbed by what she sees in the bath water. She scrubs her legs manically.*
>
> *Annie climbs out and heads straight for the secret room, wrapping up self-consciously in an old towel. Closing the door carefully and quietly behind her again. When she finally returns, she is troubled. Scared even.*
>
> *She tries to shake it off and return to routine. She dries herself carefully. She is delicate. Annie puts her clothes back on, taking care with them as though they are expensive, precious items. Not the dirty rags they truly are.*

ANNIE: Navy pleated skirt. My grey pull up socks. Crisp white shirt. Red tie and my blue blazer.

Have I got everything? Homework, Sir'll kill me if I forget that again. New school bag.

> *Annie picks up her school bag and puts it on her shoulders.*

ANNIE: Aar Mum's polished my Kickers. They look well shiny. I usually like 'em a bit more scrubby looking. But that's ok. I'll make it work.

Kick the dirty clothes under the bed... down the stairs. Grab the toast- "Er young lady, what about my kiss goodbye?" sorryyyy.

Always moaning this one.

> *Annie makes to dart out the imaginary house, but stops herself.*

ANNIE: Love you Mum. See you later.

> *She kisses her imaginary mum goodbye and starts pacing back and forth, as if mapping out a route.*

ANNIE: Out the house. Down the drive. Turn left and down the street.

> *The pain interrupts her steps. She breathes in deeply.*

ANNIE: I love that smell. Fresh air. Cut grass. Car fumes. Weather's quite good today actually. Why do British people always talk about the weather? Er, dullsville. Not far to school, 949 steps...

Mel B is back!

ANNIE: Mel B! There you are, come and have your breakfast please. Hurry up though, we'll be late for school. You know I don't like you just going off and not telling me where you're going. Get proper worried.

Mel B is scurrying dangerously close to the steel door. Annie jumps.

ANNIE: (*WHISPERING LOUDLY*) Mel B. Come away from the door please. You'll hurt yourself!

Just move away and nothing will happen. Mel?...

Annie crouches and picks up some of the remaining cheese on the floor, using it to tempt Mel B away from the door. She makes a tutting sound.

ANNIE: Look, cheese is over here, come and get it. Come on. Get away from the door you stupid animal! You'll get yourself killed! Enough vaults to kill a horse he said.

Mel!

Annie manages to move Mel B away from the door. As she does, she turns her back to it and stands up -

A loud bang from upstairs!

Annie falls back against the door, terrified. She screams and throws herself quickly away from the door and covers her head, bracing herself for an explosion.

Nothing.

Confused she manically checks herself for injuries.

ANNIE: Is everyone OK?!

Annie looks at the heavy steel door.

ANNIE: What about the booby trap?

> *She walks slowly toward the door but is interrupted by footsteps. She quickly backs away from the door, her line of thought interrupted.*
>
> *With renewed energy she makes a big effort to carry on with her routine. Back to pacing.*

ANNIE: Mum hates me to be late for school.

> *Annie picks up her school bag again. She stops to talk to someone.*

ANNIE: Tammy. Wassuup? You OK?

I said I'd meet like, loads of people before registration so they can buy their tickets for the disco. Even Mandy from the year above and her mates wanna come! And I've already sold like, 31.

> *She pauses as though listening to her invisible friend, throwing nervous looks back to the steel door.*

ANNIE: Yeah, sorry. I know. No-one believes me when I say we've organised it-

Yeah, we really need to practice our routine though. Everyone will be talking about it in school on Monday - in a good way. I really want people to be like, wow, they could BE the Spice Girls...

Yeah I know she doesn't wanna be Sporty but if she wants to do it with us she has to. I'm always Baby and you're always Posh and that's just the way it is. You know life's hard but you get over it! ...My Mums always saying that. There's no way I'm being Sporty... yeah we'll practice first break... I got P.E first, made up! Then English, Home Ec and double Art... I like PE, don't get why everyone moans-

No I don't wanna be Sporty!

Have you got drama club or you walking home today?

Great... DEFO walk home together and we can chat more about the disco.

> *Annie and Tammy walk into the imaginary school building.*

ANNIE: Up the steps through the yard and off to school...

> *She spots a crowd of people, all waiting for her and her tickets. She relaxes more, pleased and cocky. The Queen Bee.*

ANNIE: Hi Guys. You all waiting for tickets?! Yeah it's OUR disco. We booked the DJ and hall and everything- Tammy's Mum's yellow pages.

£1.50 - to cover costs. We've got finger food... every good disco has finger food Matthew! AND, there's a surprise performance as well... not saying!

BBBBRRIIIINNNNNGGGGG. Saved by the bell!

Guys I'll be in the Gym Hall first break for anyone who hasn't got their ticket yet. But you'll have to be quick, they're selling like hot toast.

> *Annie slings her bag down.*

ANNIE: Hiya Miss... so chuffed we got P.E first.

She begins to stretch but struggles as it makes the pain worse.

ANNIE: Sorry, I've got a stitch or something. Yeah, walk it off. Good idea...

Annie starts pacing, breathing deeply. She is irritated by something the imaginary teacher has said.

ANNIE: No, no, no I can do it!

Exercise is good for the body and mind isn't it? I've been practicing my cartwheels. Well good at them now. Wait 'til you see.

Sorry, one sec...

As she throws her legs in the air, pain strikes again. She falls to the floor, angry with herself.

ANNIE: See...

Miss, can I please be excused from P.E today?

Brrriiinnnggggg. English.

Annie fetches a notebook and pen from her bag - it's her diary.

ANNIE: Hi Sir.

She sits at the table and begins to write.

ANNIE: Dear Diary, heyyy me again. Had a weird sleep last night. Dreamt about Mum, except she was back with Dad. Only it didn't look like Dad, he looked like

Things have been OK... bit of a bad morning. But last night he read me some more of his poems. I love them, they don't always rhyme but they don't always have to. Some were well sad. He's definitely gonna get his big break soon, just as soon as the world stops being so "damn narrow-minded."

They'll see. One day. And then maybe he won't have to

I'm gonna make him a certificate - for "Best Poems Ever." That will make him feel better.

Brrriiiinnnggg. End of class. Later Alligator. Love, ME.

> *Annie pushes her diary to one side and fetches some knitting from her bag and sits down at the opposite side of the table. She concentrates hard as she knits. It's important she does it well.*

ANNIE: Hi Sir. A scarf Sir... a brown one. It'll keep them warm and safe wrapped up in this scarf. They protect you... from monsters under the bed, smelly boys and wicked men. I can't wait sir.

> *Suddenly the light bulb comes on. He has turned it on.*

Annie is surprised. She looks to the ceiling.

ANNIE: Thank you.

Sorry Sir, can I please be excused?

> *Annie quickly pulls her chair under the light, sprawling wide as if she's sunbathing.*
>
> *She jumps up and picks up her potted plant, bringing it underneath the light with her.*

ANNIE: Isn't that lovely Briony Petals? Soak it all up... You too Mel B.

I used to love playing out in the sun- before I came here.

I remember one summer, it was well hot. Like, Africa hot and me, Tammy and Lucy all had on our peddle pushers and tank tops and had gone to the shop to buy 99's. And when we were there the boys asked us if we wanted a water fight so funny. We filled up loadsa balloons in the park, and one got me right in the face, but I didn't even care. Just laughed. We laughed loads that day. Was so good. The boys reckoned their team won but they so didn't. We did. We kept singing 'Girls Rule' at them. And doing the Girl power sign.

Was dead good.

> *A noise from upstairs interrupts -*

For a moment, Annie sits completely still and holds her breath. Until she hears footsteps.

She jumps up and grabs her knitting and diary and hurriedly hides them back in her bag. She races to the metal bucket and hides the newspaper back underneath it.

The noise stops.

Walking towards the steel door, she listens hard.

Silence.

ANNIE: Why didn't you explode?

She studies the edges of the door without touching it. Fearful. Like a stray cat tempted by food.

She runs to the sink and searches for something.

ANNIE: Miss Philips says wood doesn't conduct electricity…

She pulls out a wooden spoon from the drawer and stands in front of the door again.

*She holds out the wooden spoon trying to summon the **courage to touch the door with it**. Again, she's* *interrupted by a thud from upstairs. Annie jumps, quickly pulling the wooden spoon away.*

Calming herself, she eventually touches the door with the spoon, just for a split second. She watches the door. Annie moves to the handle and touches it with the wooden spoon, this time holding it for 3 seconds.

Still nothing.

Annie isn't satisfied with this experiment. Braver now, she fetches a metal fork from the drawer.

Standing well back, she throws the fork at the door... and jumps back as the fork falls to the floor. Annie crawls over to the fork and tentatively touches it.

ANNIE: Not even warm...

She moves away quickly and sits back in front of the camera.

ANNIE: Table marking 4,383. Hi Mum, hope you and Jessie are OK? I tried to grab Mel B coz she was playing by the door and I fell right into it- But I'm alright? Nothing happened. I don't get it. I tested it again and it didn't explode or electrocute me- It didn't do anything. Maybe it's just on visit day- no that doesn't make any sense. He told me to stay away from it. He said if I messed with the door

I'd die a painful death and you'd never find me. It's to keep the baddies out. I don't get it, why did he-

Crap- no red light...

> *Annie picks the camera up. Pressing buttons but it fails to work.*
>
> *The pain strikes again.*
>
> *She drops the camera on the table and races to the secret room. The camera is left playing old footage. We hear Annies voice, she sounds- happier.*

ANNIE: (*O/S - CAMERA RECORDING*) Table scratching 3,998. Hi mum, hope you and Jessie are ok? Today has been a good day. Had breakfast as usual. The walk to school was good. Art class in a bit. I'm doing one of us on the beach. Like the one I did in year 4 that you put on the fridge. Hopefully better though. Can't wait for you to see it.

> *Annie groans in pain from inside the secret room.*

ANNIE: (*O/S - CAMERA RECORDING*) Mel B is getting bigger she might be a boy mouse coz she is really big now. Can't believe I ever found her scary when she first moved in. She was the size of my pinky. Oh! and I can do cartwheels now!

The tape crackles as though something else has been recorded over it.

Haunting sounds of a man having sex with a girl. Full of deep groans and high slaps.

Suddenly the tape snaps back to the original footage.

ANNIE: (*O/S - CAMERA RECORDING*) I been practicing for ages, 43 table scratches, did my first proper straight one today. In P.E. you'd be proud. I know you would

Annie is still crying from inside the secret room.

ANNIE: (*O/S - CAMERA RECORDING*) I was sick again this morning. Probably the cartwheels sounds like he's back. I miss you.

Annie's sobs from the secret room get louder. Then, silence.

Annie exits the secret room, carefully closing the door again. She picks up the camera - placing it back on the tripod. This time the red light turns on. It's recording. Annie sits in front of it. For a while she stares blankly into the lens. She finally gives up and turns it off.

Her attention snaps.

ANNIE: Briingg. Lunchtime.

Annie takes a tray from the cupboard and slides it along the dining table as though at the school canteen.

ANNIE: Sausages please. Mash and beans thanks. Can I have a bit more beans Wendy?

Sorry, Miss O'Donnell. Thank you. Is that Banana bread? Yes. Can I have two slices?

Aaar there'd better be seconds today then.

Annie picks up her tray and surveys the room. Where to sit? She smiles as though seeing her friends and sits at the dining table.

ANNIE: Banana bread day! What you smirking at? Been passing notes with Simon again? Gross. Go on then, what's it say?

So you're going to the disco with him? Thought we were gonna go in your mum's car?

No it's cute. Told you he liked you.

Annie takes her knife and fork and starts to eat the invisible food. Blowing her fork as though cooling it down and savouring every taste. She talks as though her mouth is full.

ANNIE: This is so good. It's just the right amount of hot. The mash is so creamy. Proper mash too not that packet stuff. Tastes like milky sawdust that stuff. This is amazing.

Posh sausages as well - sage and parsley. Definitely. You can just tell. It's important to eat well ladies. Body can't function properly if you don't.

I sold 7 more tickets in Home Ec. Everyone's well excited-

Pain hits her again.

ANNIE: Think we might need more sausage rolls -

The pain is impossible to ignore. She stands to put her tray away but as she turns, she is face to face with the steel door again.

Annie puts her tray down and stands in front of the door. Annie closes her eyes and reaches for the handle. She jerks her hand back. Too frightened.

ANNIE: Nothing happened before. Nothing happened before.

She runs to the sink and grabs a cloth, wrapping her hand in it. Annie tries again. Closing her eyes she holds out her hand and -

She does it!

She grabs the door handle and pulls. The door slowly OPENS.

Annie stands facing the open doorway. Breathing heavily. She slowly starts to step backwards, eyes fixed on the door.

ANNIE: You liar!

Frantically, she crawls and sits on the other side of the room, eyes still locked on the door

She hides behind the edge of the sink. Still in shock, she's breathing so fast it's hard to catch her breath. In panic she searches for things to throw at the door. Annie grabs the knife and holds it out in front of her, hands shaking.

ANNIE: Anything could get in here! I know what's out there, I know the danger. You told me you'd protect me, if I helped you with your problems. Keep me safe from all the bad stuff what happens when you grow up.

She is violently sick in the metal bucket.

ANNIE: You liar.

One loud bang from above. Annie is too upset to care.

ANNIE: Liar!

Three more BANGS! Louder and angrier this time. Annie flinches with every bang.

The light goes out. Her final punishment. Annie cries in the dark. The tears are taking over. She is having a panic attack. Annie grips the table, gulping air in between sobs and screams. Scratching at her chest.

She crawls to her bed and pulls out a brown paper bag from inside the pillowcase. She breathes into it, one hand on her chest as if guiding the rhythm of her breathing- not the first time she has suffered a panic attack.

Annie sits on the bed with the small shoe box she had earlier. She hugs the box close to her. She snaps back into her routine. Annie picks up her school bag and starts pacing again.

ANNIE: Bringg. Schools finished. Sold 13 tickets to the disco today. Have fun at drama club Tammy...

Tammy? You're the bestest friend a girl could ever ask for.

Annie savours the moment before carrying on with her journey.

ANNIE: In the corridor, about to walk home.

Kevin is by the main door- who's he waiting for?

He's smiling at me. I love his dimples. And his eyes. Sparkly blue. Like the sea in Crete that summer. And his dopey fringe, gelled into spikes like a little spider. Spider of dreaminess.

He's walking over to me. I've got a jumpy feeling in my tummy. Act cool

Hiya Kev... yeah I'm OK. Mr Banes just gave us a load of homework

Don't talk about homework- what you standing here for? The disco? Yeah you want a ticket?... course I'm going you dope, it's my disco!

He looks embarrassed. He's so cute! You want me to go with you?

I'd really like that.

> *Movement from upstairs. Annie freezes and listens. The sound of a door opening and closing. And a car starting. He has gone out.*

ANNIE: He's gone. Mel B he's gone out!

He's going to miss his visit again. He-

> *She points at the steel door.*

ANNIE: He doesn't know we know!

No. No. He knows everything. He's testing me. It's dangerous out there

> *Annie quickly pushes the table and chairs up against the door, closing it and forming a blockade. She fetches the newspaper from under the metal bucket and flattens it out on the ground next to her, reading.*

ANNIE: People are nasty out there.

Terrorists. Kids with knives and guns. Gangs with their hoods up, prowling like lions looking for prey. Addicts with dirty needles and drugs. Fast cars. Dogs what eat you coz their owners told them to. Cancer in your Diet Coke.

And Michael Jackson's in court for doing sexual abuse to a 13-year old boy.

Even the King of Pop does bad things Mel B. Do you think the Evil Spirits got MJ too?

> *Annie jerks her head up listening.*

ANNIE: I know that's what you think Katie!

> *She moves to the wall where she spoke to Katie earlier and bangs on the wall.*

ANNIE: Just shut up will you!

I know you don't like him, I know you don't wanna be here but he said it's for the best, it's for our own good. I don't need you butting in every 10 seconds!

I know he lied about the door.

But what if it's true about outside? Yeah, my mum always looked after me too.

Annie sits in front of the camera and turns it on.

ANNIE: Table scratching 4,383. Mum. Hope you and Jessie are OK? The door's not locked. It's open. I don't understand? Has it always been?

Sometimes I pretend he has other basement rooms where he keeps other little girls, like Katie. And Janey and Emma before her.

Not coz I want other people to feel sad, just, so I can talk to them.

It was nice to have someone know how it feels. What it's like.

And that way, when he says I have to be here so he won't do it to other little girls I can understand, coz he won't do it to Katie.

I hate being the only one. I'm so lonely down here.

I know I can talk to you but sometimes I just wish you would reply. Why don't you reply?

He said you don't have a camera but what about all the home videos we used to make?

> *She glances at the steel door and then back to the camera.*

ANNIE: No...

> *Annie jumps up and inspects the camera.*

ANNIE: W-W-W Dot... W-W-W Dot.

The net. Into-net. You said Mum gets my messages by into-net. By W-W-W Dot... where is W-W-W Dot?!

> *She finds another button.*

ANNIE: Eject.

"Don't press Eject little girl. Press eject and the camera will blow, just like the door."

Why don't you want me to press Eject?

> *A fresh wave of pain hits her.*

ANNIE: Please don't do this...

Pain strikes again.

She heads towards the secret room. Her hand on the handle but she can't bring herself to open it. Annie slumps to the floor and starts to cry.

ANNIE: Please don't leave me. I need you more than ever. I'll do anything. I promise I won't do any more cartwheels. I shouldn't have done them. I'm sorry. Please.

I can't make it stop.

The pain is too much. She pulls open the door to the secret room and goes inside, shutting it behind her.

She's in there an age, out of sight as we hear her pain and cries.

Finally, she exits, quickly walking out of the room in a daze. Behind her, the secret room door is left open with the light on revealing a toilet.

There is blood on the floor and a nest of bloody tissues.

Annie has miscarried.

She stands motionless. In front of her is Briony Petals. She stares silently at the plant. As if seeing it for the first time.

ANNIE: You're a dead fucking plant!

She staggers to her school bag and puts it back on. She snaps back into her imaginary school day. Pacing back and forth.

ANNIE: Walking home. Hate walking by myself. Can't believe Kevin asked me to the disco. He could have gone with any of the girls in Year 7. We can go to the cinema and bowling.

Tammy and Simon, me and Kev.

Oh my god.

What if he wants to kiss me?! Tammy says it's gross.

If Kevin wants to kiss me, I'm gonna to do it. Hope he likes my dress. It's from C & A, dark purple with pink spaghetti straps. Mandy from the year above says its aaall about spaghetti straps.

There's my house. Just a few more steps. Only 2 hours until the disco. Just enough time to get all my butterfly clips in.

Key in the door. Muum! Guess what-guess what?!

No response. Annie looks around her. She spots something on the kitchen table. A note from her mum.

ANNIE: "Working late Princess, I've left you £5 on the dresser and you can use my mascara this once if you promise to put the lid back on. You'll have to walk by yourself to the disco. Love, Mummy Bear"

She stares sadly at the toilet.

She takes her school bag off and slides to the floor. Time to say goodbye.

ANNIE: I would of loved you well loads, you know that don't you?

We wouldn't have minded being down here, coz we'd have each other. It wouldn't matter about windows coz I could tell you all the stories about outside. We could pretend we're at school, plan the disco and when you were big you could be Baby, Mel B could be Scary, Briony Petals could be Ginger and I could be Posh.

I could teach you gymnastics and reading and make you loads of nice clothes. I promise you would have been OK.

I wanted to be your Mummy. You would ask loads about your Nana and I'd tell you how warm she was. How her cuddles always made me feel safe and whenever I cut my knee or banged my elbow, she'd give it a magic kiss better and the pain would just go away. Real life magic. I can't do magic but I would have made your pain go away. Everyday.

I tried to. I hope you didn't feel any pain. I didn't mean for it to happen. I already lost your brother and sisters.

But I'm going to make it right. You deserve better than being stuck down here.

So do I. Sleep tight my Baby Bear.

> *After a moment she moves to the camera. Slamming it on the chair.*

ANNIE: What happens when you press Eject...?

> *She paces to the other side of the basement, standing, watching it.*

ANNIE: The door was a lie. You do bad things, just like out there.

You said Mum gets my messages - you send them to her.

> *She moves to the camera. She picks it up and holds it away from her. Her finger hovers over the Eject button. Turning her face away, Annie closes her eyes and takes a deep breath*
>
> *...and presses EJECT.*

Silence. Then a click as the tape deck opens.

She looks at it, confused. And carefully takes the tape out to study it.

ANNIE: I don't get it.

Where are all my messages? Where's the into-net? What happens when the tape runs out?

I've made 1,279 messages to my mum since you said I could use the camera. That's hours and hours.

She moves to the cupboard under the sink and pulls everything out, searching for more tapes.

ANNIE: I used to make mix tapes for Tammy. Megamix 2000 volumes 1 to 11. You could fit 12 songs on each side of the tape, after that it'd just record over stuff. So there can't just be one tape. Where are all the other tapes? What have you done with my messages?

She runs back to the camera and finds the Play button.

ANNIE: You promised Mum knew I was OK!

Annie presses Play and watches the footage.

ANNIE: (*O/S - CAMERA RECORDING*) I've been drawing you a lot lately mum. It scares me that it's getting harder to remember your face. I try so hard to hold on to you-

> *Annie presses fast forward. She plays another part of the tape.*

ANNIE: (*O/S - CAMERA RECORDING*) Happy birthday dear mummyyy, happy birthday to youuu-

> *The voice stops and the tape crackles as though something else has been recorded over it.*
>
> *We hear the noise of a man having sex with a girl. Annie watches, she's never seen herself being attacked. She closes her eyes in shame.*

ANNIE: (*WHISPERING*) Stop it. Stop it.

> *Annie slaps the camera off. She stumbles over to the cupboard under the sink and hides the camera.*
>
> *She slowly washes her hands trying to regain control. She then scrubs her arms, her face. Getting faster and more manic.*
>
> *Suddenly! The front doorbell rings.*
>
> *It's visit time. Annie freezes, listening. She slowly moves away from the steel door. The doorbell sounds*

again. Annie opens her mouth - but no sound will come out.

A heavy knock on the front door. She steps tentatively towards the sound.

A faint voice on a radio. Then footsteps and eventually the sound of a car pulling away. She has missed her chance. She looks around desperately and fetches her diary and reads back a previous entry.

ANNIE: The world is such a cruel place. Don't they see the pain they cause?

He cried again today, I hate seeing him like this. If only they'd just listen to his poems, he wouldn't feel so rejected and then the Evil Spirits wouldn't make him hurt me.

She flicks the pages and reads some more.

ANNIE: Had breakfast as usual. He was talking about how awful this stupid shop assistant was in the supermarket, he was so angry he didn't even finish his cereal. Some girls can be right bitc-

Annie turns the page.

ANNIE: He got me a present today. The prettiest plant in the world. I'm gonna call her Briony Petals. He says if I look after her, he'll let me plant her in the garden.

And if I keep watering her she'll grow big and strong just like him.

> *She reads on but this time to herself, flicking through the pages faster and faster.*

ANNIE: No name... no name... no name!

You don't let me write my own name. You won't even let me say it.

You want me to stay scared of out there. Forget who I am.

> *With renewed bravery she walks to the table in front of the steel door. She starts to pull away the furniture. Clearing the entrance to the door.*
>
> *It's just her and the door again.*
>
> *She puts her hand on the handle and wills herself to open it. She stands in front of the open door. Proud.*
>
> *She spins around looking for something.*

ANNIE: Mel B? Where are you? Mel B?

I'm leaving this place Mel B. We've got to clear up the crumbs, no-one to protect you once I'm gone. He can't know about you.

She busies herself cleaning the floor.

Suddenly - Mel B darts through the open door.

ANNIE: Mel B?! Come back! It's not safe!

Annie gets to all fours and tries to beckon Mel B back. Her eyes follow the mouse up the stairs to the exit.

ANNIE: Mel B?

Be careful.

You did it.

You did it! You escaped! You flippin' did it!

Suddenly she springs into action, picking up her school bag. She places cans of food in her bag.

ANNIE: I'll run for miles if I have to. It doesn't matter how far away. I'm coming home. It's all over. You won't have to worry any more Mum.

You'll still want won't you? You're not ashamed?

She stops packing.

ANNIE: But you don't know what I've done. How nasty and dirty-

She snaps back to her imagination.

ANNIE: Got my dress on.

Body glitter on my shoulders so I sparkle in the lights. I hope Kevin likes it.

She paces the room again.

ANNIE: I usually hate walking by myself but today I don't mind. I need to think of a good joke for when I see him. Grandad says if you make him laugh he'll love you forever.

I'm on that well long street. Big trees and bushes on each side. With dark green shiny leaves and little flowers pokin' out some of the bushes. Pink and purple. Just like my dress.

I've got my jelly sandals on. The ones with the high heel, feel well grown up. Mum would say glamorous. Turn the corner.

At the end of the road there's a white van parked up. The man's standing by it, smoking. Gross. I watch him as I walk.

Is he moving house? No building work going on. I kinda want to cross the road so I don't walk past him. Stupid. Spooking myself out like I always do, if Tammy was here she'd just laugh at me-

Annie stops pacing.

ANNIE: I should have crossed the road.

He grabbed me so fast I didn't even see him move. One arm round my waist and one over my mouth. I tried to scream but no sound would come out. I threw my hands out to hold onto something but all I got was the leaves. It must have been raining coz they're wet. I remember the feel of them. They broke away in my hand.

It's so dark in here. I can't breathe. It smells of staleness. I can hear the blood pounding in my ears.

Kevin will think I didn't want to come. He won't see my dress. He won't tell me I look pretty.

You never got my messages did you Mum? Briony Petals isn't here anymore. And-

> *She picks up the small shoe box still on the bed and looks inside. She carefully lifts from it; a mouse trap with a dead mouse caught in it.*
>
> *Mel B.*
>
> *Annie listens intently. She picks up a chair and bangs it on the floor. She waits.*
>
> *No movement. No angry banging. He's definitely out.*

It's time to leave. She springs into action, packing her bag.

ANNIE: If that door at the top of those stairs is locked it's just made of wood so I can kick it through. He's not back yet. But he won't be long so I'm gonna have to think quick. Be quick.

After that, I'm in the main part of the house, the kitchen I think. I just have to run through to the hall and there's the front door. That WILL be locked. But I can break a window.

Can have a new life, instead of remembering the old one. Say my name, write my name. Be me again.

Stop listening to your excuses. How it's never your fault. You don't just lie to me, you lie to yourself. I can still be found. You were lost a long time ago.

She walks to the steel door.

ANNIE: I'm going home. I'm not scared anymore. You will never hurt me or my family again. Back out the way I came in. 4,383 days ago...

She stops.

ANNIE: And let's get one thing straight...

Annie takes the knife and scratching into the table, writes HIM a note.

ANNIE: MY. NAME. IS -

The steel door SLAMS shut and LOCKS.

Annie stands perfectly still. Her back to the door.

Silence fills the room. She doesn't move. Eventually she turns and stares at the door. Annie takes the wooden spoon to the door to test it again. But can't bring herself to try.

She takes the camera from under the sink and set's it back up on the tripod. She sits in front of it.

ANNIE: Table scratching 4,383. Hi Mum. Me again. Hope you and Jessie are ok?

Won't be long. Any day now.

Can't wait to see you. So much to tell you. I miss you.

Annie stares blankly into the camera.
Staring at nothing. Smiling at nothing.

THE END
Author's note: The actress should remain in character throughout the applause. No bow. No stage exit.